ABUNDANT TRUTH INTERNATIONAL MINISTRIES

Apostolic Ministry Revival Series

THE APOSTOLIC PARADIGM SHIFT

Examining the Coming Reformation of Apostles and Apostolic Ministry

Roderick Levi Evans

The Apostolic Paradigm Shift

Examining the Coming Reformation of Apostles and Apostolic Ministry

All Rights Reserved ©2012 by Roderick L. Evans

No part of this book may be reproduced or transmitted in any form or by any means, graphic, electronic, or mechanical, including photocopying, recording, taping, or by any information storage or retrieval system, without the permission in writing from the publisher.

Front & Back Cover Designs by Abundant Truth Publishing, U.S.A. All rights reserved.

Abundant Truth Publishing
an imprint of Abundant Truth International Ministries

For information address:
Abundant Truth International
P.O. Box 126
Camden, NC 27921

ISBN 13: 978-1-60141-330-7

Printed in the United States of America

Unless otherwise indicated, all of the scripture quotations are taken from the Authorized King James Version of the Bible. Scripture quotations marked with NIV are taken from the New International Version of the Bible. Scripture quotations marked with NASV are taken from the New American Standard Version of the Bible. Scripture quotations marked with Amplified are taken from the Amplified Bible.

Contents

Preface
Introduction

Chapter 1 – The Apostolic Paradigm Shift   1

Matthias: The Chosen Apostle   6

Matthias: The Silent Apostle   8

Matthias: The Processed Apostle   10

Matthias: The Prepared Apostle   12

Matthias: The Committed Apostle   16

Matthias: The Seer- Apostle   19

Chapter 2 – The Apostolic Representation   25

Joseph: The Called Apostolic   29

Joseph: The Secret Apostolic   31

Contents (cont.)

Joseph: The Processed Apostolic	33
Joseph: The Prepared Apostolic	36
Joseph: The Committed Apostolic	40
Joseph: The Prophetic Apostolic	42

Chapter 3 - The Apostolic Expression — 49

The Great Outpouring	52
The Great Revelation	54

Chapter 4 - The Apostolic Administration — 59

The Great Outpouring	61
The Great Commission	63

Contents (cont.)

Chapter 5 – The Apostolic Reformation   **73**

Reformation of Love   76

Reformation of the Miraculous   77

Reformation of Disciples   79

Preface

Apostles and apostolic ministry are important to the furtherance of the Kingdom of God and the Church. It is my prayer that the information presented in this work will prepare believers for the reformation that will occur in the demonstration of the apostolic ministry.

Numerous works have been produced which highlight the ministry of the apostle. However, the information in this book will bring believers into a greater understanding of the shift coming to apostles and apostolic ministry

Roderick Levi Evans

Introduction

As the disciples waited for the promise of the Faithe; that is, the baptism of the Holy Ghost, they cast lots to discover who would replace Judas. When the qualified candidate was selected, they continued in prayer.

After this, the Holy Spirit came upon those gathered in the upper room, and they instantly became powerful witnesses of the Resurrection. Souls were converted and the new converts were confirmed in the faith. The Apostolic Ministry Revival

Series was developed to demonstrate how God is bringing a restoration and revival to apostles and apostolic ministry for an end time expansion of the Kingdom of God and establishing of believers in the faith.

In this publication:

Controversy over the gifts and ministries of the Spirit has abounded for centuries. Various scholars have taught that there was a cessation of the gifts and ministries. More specifically, they affirm that the ministry of the Apostle is no longer in operation nor valid. However, in recent years, a resurgence of the operation and demonstration of this ministry occurred.

Traditional and Non-traditional churches, alike, have experienced the visitation of God through the Holy Spirit.

Since the emergence and acceptance of the ministries and gifts of the Holy Spirit, various authors have written concerning this phenomenon.

In spite of this, many in the Church, presently, do not understand the functions and operations of, namely, the office of the Apostle. Even in organizations and denominations that consider this ministry valid today, comprehension is oftentimes elementary.

Where there is no clear understanding, individuals become vulnerable to deception and error. Many apostles have abused their ministries and authority. Therefore, the Lord is going to send a reformation in the midst of the Church. It is designed to bring purity again to the apostolic office. Not only in the execution of this ministry, but also in the perspective for which it is received.

In the second book of this series, we will show from the biblical account of how the early Church experienced an apostolic revival and restoration, which impacted the influence and advancement of the gospel of Jesus Christ and establish individuals in the New Testament faith.

THE APOSTOLIC PARRADIGM SHIFT — Examining the Coming Reformation of Apostles and Apostolic Ministry

-Chapter 1-

The Apostolic Paradigm Shift

THE APOSTOLIC PARRADIGM SHIFT

Examining the Coming Reformation of Apostles and Apostolic Ministry

In the first book, we discussed how the apostolic paradigm shift began with a restoration of the acceptance, work, and character of the apostolic ministry through an apostolic revolution.

After this restoration, an apostolic rejection proceeded from the Lord against disobedient and self-willed apostles throughout the centuries. This led to the need for reformation.

We also discussed how that established apostles should intercede and prepare the way for the apostolic paradigm shift to take place. One must understand that the apostolic paradigm unfolds as a company of apostles comes forward in the Kingdom of God.

Continuing our examination of the events in the upper room from the first book of this series, we discover that the choosing of Matthias (to stand with the other eleven) reflects the present-day apostolic transition.

As we consider the man, Matthias, we will understand the fullness of God's present move It is within this apostolic personality that we find the heart of the apostolic paradigm shift. Peter requested that the disciples present find men who met certain qualifications to replace Judas.

Wherefore of these men which have companied with us all the time that the Lord Jesus went in and out among us, Beginning from the baptism of John, unto that same day that he was taken up from us, must one be ordained to be a witness with us of his resurrection. (Acts 1:21-22)

When they had looked among them, they found two men, which met all of these qualifications: Matthias and Joseph.

And they appointed two, Joseph called Barsabas, who was surnamed Justus, and Matthias. (Acts 1:23)

After prayer, the lot fell upon Matthias as the Lord's choice for apostleship. When we examine more closely the calling and ordination to the apostolic ministry, we discover how the apostolic paradigm shift will operate.

Matthias: The Chosen Apostle

Matthias was chosen by the Lord to stand with the apostles. He did not exalt or endorse himself. Yet, the Lord made clear that he was His choice. The disciples could recognize the signs of apostleship, but a clear approval from the Lord had to accompany it.

From this, we discover that the company of apostles that are emerging will have the Lord's seal upon them. Like Matthias, God has reserved them until this present time to place them in position.

So the last shall be first, and the first last: for many be called, but few chosen. (Matthew 20:16)

The apostles coming will not be stubborn, self-willed, or prideful, but in *humility*, will they receive the Lord's calling and walk therein.

Matthias: The Silent Apostle

We have no record of Matthias in any of the Gospels. We discover that one of the qualifications for apostleship was that he had to have been with Jesus from His baptism until His ascension. Matthias remained *faithful* to Christ without recognition or fame.

The apostles ushering in the apostolic paradigm walk in the way of Matthias. They have been *faithful* to the Lord in secret.

Moreover it is required in stewards, that a man be found faithful. (I Corinthians 4:2)

They have maintained godly lifestyles and have spent time developing their relationship with Him. They did not do it for a position or ministry, but because they were dedicated to the Lord.

Matthias followed the Lord for His entire earthly ministry without any position. This prepared him for the future ministry. The emerging apostles have served because they were committed to the Lord. In turn, He will reveal them to the world as He did Matthias.

Matthias: The Processed Apostle

Matthias walked with Christ from the baptism of John. Though he was not a part of the inner twelve, he, too, had to leave all and follow Christ. He had to be present in the places where Christ traveled and ministered.

Undoubtedly, he experienced some difficulties and hardships when he made a decision to follow Christ. Thus, he was prepared to endure the hardships that come with apostolic ministry.

The apostles of the apostolic

paradigm shift are individuals who have gone through the Lord's breaking and molding process. Matthias had to witness Jesus' baptism from John.

John's baptism was one to repentance. This demonstrates that the emerging apostles will have forsaken unrighteous and ungodly lifestyles and ambitions. They are apostles who are willing to call men to repentance as they walk in repentance from dead works.

The coming apostles will be individuals whom the Lord has allowed to suffer great rejection, persecution, failures, and setbacks to ensure that they will remain humble in service. They will appreciate the apostolic call, bringing honor to God and respect for the office.

But the God of all grace, who hath called us unto his eternal glory by Christ Jesus, after that ye have suffered a while, make you perfect, stablish, strengthen, settle you. (I Peter 5:10)

Matthias: The Prepared Apostle

Matthias was present; according to all of the qualifications presented by Peter, the whole time Jesus went in and out among them. Therefore, he received teaching and instructions from Christ. He may have been among the seventy that were sent out by Christ.

After these things the Lord appointed other seventy also, and sent them two and two before his face into every city and place, whither he himself would come. (Luke 10:1)

If this is true, which is highly probable, Matthias and the others were not sent out without instructions for service and an understanding of the kingdom.

The apostolic individuals coming from obscurity are taught of the Lord. They will minister with sound doctrine and understanding. Many of them will have a similar testimony to Paul's. He declared that he received a revelation of the Gospel from Christ.

> *But I certify you, brethren, that the gospel which was preached of me is not after man. For I neither received it of man, neither was I taught it, but by the revelation of Jesus Christ. (Galatians 1:11-12)*

This means that these apostles will not preach from the wisdom of men. They have sat at the Lord's feet and received the necessary tools for ministry. They stand prepared to declare fully the mysteries of the Kingdom of God.

They will only present that which is clearly revealed through the scriptures and revelation of the Spirit. They will not preach about themselves or ministries, but only things pertaining to the Kingdom of God and His Christ.

Their ministries in the word will bring men back into the purity of the faith. They will present Christ as Lord. Their preaching and teaching will not be laced with covetousness and hypocrisy. They will lead men and women to the risen Christ. Their message will prepare men for the coming of the Lord. Remember, all New Testament ministry will point to the second coming of Christ.

Matthias: The Committed Apostle

Matthias also demonstrated a commitment to the Lord and to the brethren. Peter stated the apostle who replaced Judas had to have companied with them all the time while Christ was in the earth. Not only did Matthias follow the Lord, but also he had fellowship with the other disciples. This revealed his connection with other followers of the Lord.

The apostolic paradigm shift will reveal apostles who have a love for the Church. They will not be lone rangers. They will promote unity and love among the Body of Christ.

Some apostles use apostolic ministry to divide the Church and to gain a following. The coming apostles will demonstrate a love for the brethren.

Their commitment to the Church will mirror the sentiment of Paul when he stated,

> *Behold, the third time I am ready to come to you; and I will not be burdensome to you: for I seek not yours, but you: for the children ought not to lay up for the parents, but the parents for the children. And I will very gladly spend and be spent for you... (II Corinthians 12:14-15a)*

Paul revealed his love for the saints at Corinth. He was willing to give all that he had for their success in the kingdom of

God. The apostolic paradigm shift will produce apostles who are selfless and willing to lay down their lives (ministries, time, prayer, and gifts) for the Body of Christ.

Matthias: The Seer-Apostle

Another qualification listed by Peter was that the individual had to have seen Jesus ascend back into heaven (solidifying the witness of the resurrection). Matthias was present when the Lord gave final instruction and teachings ending with His reception into heaven. He had an eyewitness experience of the Lord in His glory. For this cause, he, like the others, can be called 'seer-apostles.'

The term 'seer-apostle' reveals the spiritual insight and revelation of the emerging apostolic company. First, they will see the Lord for who He is. Their perception and presentation of Christ will be genuine in presentation and application. They have a revelation of Christ. Second, they will have spiritual insight into the plans and purposes of God in the earth.

Thirdly, they will have a proper perception of who they are and their place in the Lord's service. Finally, the revelatory gifts of the Spirit will manifest in them consistently and accurately. Many of the coming apostles will have ministries similar to John, the Beloved. They will have a pronounced prophetic ministry complimenting their primary roles as apostles.

The ordination of Matthias marked a change in the apostolic ministry of the day. It marked the beginning of change. Matthias is the personality of the apostolic paradigm shift. His example will be emulated in the apostles of the apostolic

THE APOSTOLIC PARRADIGM SHIFT
Examining the Coming Reformation of Apostles and Apostolic Ministry

paradigm shift. The apostolic paradigm shift will produce apostles of character and integrity, which sets the stage for a move of God in the earth.

Before examining the effects of the present and ensuing apostolic paradigm shift, we want to examine another personality in the apostolic paradigm shift.

Another man possessed the necessary qualifications to replace Judas as Matthias, but he was not chosen to take part in the ministry of the apostles: the disciple named Joseph.

THE APOSTOLIC PARRADIGM SHIFT
Examining the Coming Reformation of Apostles and Apostolic Ministry

Notes:

THE APOSTOLIC PARRADIGM SHIFT
Examining the Coming Reformation of Apostles and Apostolic Ministry

-Chapter 2-

The Apostolic Representation

THE APOSTOLIC PARRADIGM SHIFT

Examining the Coming Reformation of Apostles and Apostolic Ministry

Matthias reflects the heart of the apostolic paradigm shift. His replacement of Judas reveals God's work of removing apostles who have rejected His leadership.

In turn, He is filling their positions with apostles of character and integrity.

The upper room events, however, reveal that another individual stood out among the brethren as a candidate for apostleship. Again, it was the disciple named Joseph.

And they appointed two, Joseph called Barsabas, who was surnamed

Justus, and Matthias. (Acts 1:23, Emphasis mine)

When I considered this, I asked God for wisdom. If Matthias represented the company of apostles coming forth, what did the disciples' recommendation of Joseph represent?

The wisdom of God revealed that Joseph represented a company of apostolic individuals who would emerge throughout the Body of Christ. These individuals would not be apostles, but they (like Joseph) will meet the qualifications for apostolic ministry.

This company of believers will possess an apostolic anointing upon their lives, which enhances their service to the Lord. Joseph becomes then the personality of the coming apostolic representation in the Body of Christ.

Since he met the same qualifications as Matthias, an examination of his example is necessary to understand how the apostolic representation will operate in the Church.

Joseph: The Called Apostolic

The apostles chose Joseph as a candidate for apostleship. We discover that the Lord had chosen Matthias. We have no record of Joseph feeling rejected or causing division among the disciples. He accepted that the Lord had not called him as an apostle of the Lamb.

From this, we discover that the company of apostolic individuals will be comfortable in their service to the Lord. They will not seek fame, fortune, position, or title.

They, like Joseph, will continue to serve the Lord without titles. They understand that God has given them a measure in the apostolic and will not operate in a manner reserved for apostles only. They understand Jesus' words,

> *...for there be many called, but few chosen. (Matthew 20:16)*

The apostolic representation coming will not be stubborn, self-willed, or prideful, but in *humility*, will they work supporting those who stand on the front lines of ministry.

Joseph: The Secret Apostolic

We have no record of Joseph, like Matthias, in any of the Gospels. Again, one of the qualifications for apostleship was that he had to have been with Jesus from

His baptism until His ascension. Joseph remained *faithful* to Christ without recognition or fame.

The apostolic individuals have been *faithful* to the Lord in secret. However, their work in the Body will bless countless others.

Moreover, it is required in stewards, that a man be found faithful. (I Corinthians 4:2)

They have maintained Christ-centered lifestyles and have spent time developing their relationships with Him. They did not do it for a position or title, but because they were committed to Christ. Joseph followed the Lord throughout His ministry without any position.

This revealed his personal dedication to Christ. The emerging apostolic individuals have served because they were committed to the Lord. In turn, He will anoint and use them greatly in the Church and world.

Joseph: The Processed Apostolic

Joseph walked with Christ from the baptism of John. Though he was not a part of the inner twelve, he, too, had to leave all and follow Christ. He had to be present in the many places where Christ traveled and ministered. Undoubtedly, he experienced some difficulties and hardships when he decided to follow the Savior. He prepared himself to endure the hardships that came with service to Christ.

The people of the apostolic representation have experienced the Lord's breaking and molding process. Joseph witnessed Jesus' baptism from John.

John's baptism was one to repentance. This demonstrates that the emerging apostolic representation will have allowed the teachings of Christ to break down unrighteous and ungodly lifestyles and ambitions. They are willing to challenge other believers in their walks with the Lord and compel men to repent of their sins to follow Jesus.

The coming apostolic individuals will be individuals whom the Lord has allowed to suffer great rejection, persecution, failures, and setbacks.

They will have testimonies of God's deliverance from grievous trials and tests. They, too, will appreciate the apostolic anointing upon their lives, bringing honor to God.

> *But the God of all grace, who hath called us Unto his eternal glory by Christ Jesus, after that ye have suffered a while, make you perfect, stablish, strengthen, settle you. (I Peter 5:10)*

Joseph: The Prepared Apostolic

Joseph, like Matthias, was present; according to the qualifications presented by Peter, the whole time Jesus went in and out among them. Therefore, he received teaching and instructions from

Christ. He also may have been among the seventy that were sent out by Christ.

> *After these things the Lord appointed other seventy also, and sent them two and two before his face into every city and place, whither he himself would come. (Luke 10:1)*

If this is true, which is highly probable, Matthias, Joseph, and the others were not sent without instructions for service and an understanding of the kingdom. The apostolic individuals coming from obscurity are also taught of the Lord.

They will minister with sound doctrine and understanding. Many of them will have a similar testimony to Paul's. He declared that he received a revelation of the Gospel from Christ.

> *But I certify you, brethren, that the gospel which was preached of me is not after man. For I neither received it of man, neither was I taught it, but by the revelation of Jesus Christ. (Galatians 1:11-12)*

This means that these apostolic individuals will know how to rightly interpret and explain the scriptures. They have sat at the Lord's feet and received for Him. They stand prepared to fully declare the Gospel of the Kingdom of God.

They will communicate that which is clearly revealed through the scriptures and revelation of the Spirit. They will not promote themselves or falsehood, but only things pertaining to the Kingdom of God and His Christ.

Their presentation of the word will help to bring people back into the purity of the faith. They will present Christ as Lord. Their doctrine will be solid, not tainted with philosophy and vanity.

They will lead men and women to the risen Christ. They will prepare the hearts of men for Christ's coming.

Joseph: The Committed Apostolic

Joseph also demonstrated a commitment to the Lord and to the brethren. Peter stated the one who replaced Judas had to have companied with them all the time while Christ was in the earth.

Not only did Joseph follow the Lord, but also he had fellowship with the other disciples, like Matthias. This revealed his connection with the other followers of the

Lord.

The apostolic paradigm shift reveals apostolic individuals who have a love for their brothers and sisters in the Lord. They will not be selfish and reclusive. They will promote unity and love among the Body of Christ.

The coming apostolic representation will demonstrate a love for the Church. The apostolic representation will produce individuals who are selfless and willing to lay down their lives (ministries, time, prayer, finances, service, and gifts) for the brethren.

Joseph: The Prophetic Apostolic

The final qualification listed by Peter was that the individual had to have seen Jesus ascend back into heaven (solidifying the witness of the resurrection).

Joseph was present when the Lord gave final instruction and teachings ending with Him reception into heaven. He had an eyewitness experience of the Lord in His glory. Because of this, we discover that Joseph represents an apostolic representation with a prophetic touch.

The term prophetic reveals the

spiritual insight and revelation of the emerging apostolic individuals. First, they will see the Lord for who He is. Their perception and presentation of Christ will be genuine in presentation and application. They have a revelation of Christ. Second, they will have spiritual insight into the plans and purposes of God in the earth.

Thirdly, they will have a proper perception of who they are and their place in the Lord's service. Finally, the revelatory gifts of the Spirit will manifest in them consistently and accurately. Many of those included in the apostolic representation will be like the daughters of Philip.

The daughters had recognized prophetic gifts, though they were not called prophets (some translations try to identify them as prophets, yet, most manuscripts only suggest that they prophesied only). Those in the apostolic representation will have valid prophetic gifts complimenting the apostolic anointing.

The disciples' recognition of Joseph's qualifications reveals the level of service and commitment those in the apostolic representation will possess. The apostolic paradigm shift will make its greatest impact upon the Church and the world as the apostolic individuals arise and stand to serve along with the apostles.

THE APOSTOLIC PARRADIGM SHIFT Examining the Coming Reformation of Apostles and Apostolic Ministry

Notes:

THE APOSTOLIC PARRADIGM SHIFT
Examining the Coming Reformation of Apostles and Apostolic Ministry

-Chapter 3-

The Apostolic Expression

THE APOSTOLIC PARRADIGM SHIFT — Examining the Coming Reformation of Apostles and Apostolic Ministry

THE APOSTOLIC PARRADIGM SHIFT — Examining the Coming Reformation of Apostles and Apostolic Ministry

For many years, prophets and other ministers have predicted the coming of a revival that will have global implications. These prophecies reveal that revivals will happen in many places around the world simultaneously. It will mark one of the Lord's final calls to repentance before the end of all things.

Though we have seen some notable revivals take place in recent decades, none seemed to match the Spirit's revelation of the revivals to come. There is still an end-time outpouring of the Spirit to come.

Repent ye therefore, and be converted, that your sins may be blotted out, when the times of refreshing shall come from the presence of the Lord. (Acts 3:19)

The Great Outpouring

After Matthias was ordained to stand with the other apostles, something extraordinary happened.

And they gave forth their lots; and the lot fell upon Matthias; and he was numbered with the eleven apostles. (Acts 1:26)

Shortly afterwards, the next event

recorded was the outpouring of the Holy Spirit. The promised Spirit did not come until after the apostolic was restored. This reveals that the apostolic paradigm shift marks the beginning of the fulfillment of the modern-day prophecies of great revival. This is what is demonstrated from the events in the upper room.

> *And suddenly there came a sound from heaven as of a rushing mighty wind, and it filled all the house where they were sitting. And there appeared unto them cloven tongues like as of fire, and it sat upon each of*

them. And they were all filled with the Holy Ghost, and began to speak with other tongues, as the Spirit gave them utterance. (Acts 2:2-4)

The Great Revelation

The outpouring of the Holy Spirit did not only signify the birth of the Church, but it ushered in a time when the revelation of God would abound in those that served him.

When Peter stood to address the crowd, he told them what was the major by-product of the Spirit's outpouring.

But this is that which was spoken by

the prophet Joel; And it shall come to pass in the last days, saith God, I will pour out of my Spirit upon all flesh: and your sons and your daughters shall prophesy, and your young men shall see visions, and your old men shall dream dreams: And on my servants and on my handmaidens I will pour out in those days of my Spirit; and they shall prophesy. (Acts 2:16-18)

The major result of the Spirit's outpouring was revelation; namely, prophetic utterances, dreams, and visions.

If the apostolic paradigm shift of today will prepare the way for an outpouring, then we can safely conclude that there will be increase in the supernatural revelation of God and Jesus in the Church. Prophecy, dreams, visions, and the like will be in abundance to empower the Church for service.

Notes:

THE APOSTOLIC PARRADIGM SHIFT

Examining the Coming Reformation of Apostles and Apostolic Ministry

-Chapter 4-

The Apostolic Administration

THE APOSTOLIC PARRADIGM SHIFT Examining the Coming Reformation of Apostles and Apostolic Ministry

This chapter is entitled the apostolic revelation. This does not refer to revelation from apostolic individuals, but it refers to the Church's corporate apostolic administration which reveals Christ to the world.

The Great Outpouring

The outpouring of the Spirit and prophetic revelation makes this possible. The man that talked with John on Patmos reveals this truth when he states,

> *... for the testimony of Jesus is the spirit of prophecy. (Revelation 19:10)*

The Holy Spirit comes with the spirit

of prophecy. The Church needs the prophetic revelation of the Spirit to give the proper testimony of Jesus. It is through the spirit of prophecy that the apostolic commission is fulfilled.

> *Go ye therefore, and teach all nations, baptizing them in the name of the Father, and of the Son, and of the Holy Ghost: Teaching them to observe all things whatsoever I have commanded you: and, lo, I am with you always, even unto the end of the world. Amen. (Matthew 28:19-20)*

THE APOSTOLIC PARRADIGM SHIFT — Examining the Coming Reformation of Apostles and Apostolic Ministry

The Great Commission

The apostolic revelation that is produced by the apostolic paradigm shift propels the Church into success with the four-fold administration of Great Commission.

The commission should produce four distinct phenomena:

I. An increase in evangelism

II. An expansion of the kingdom of God

III. Mature disciples

IV. Greater faith of the church

Increased Evangelism (Go ye...)

The apostolic paradigm shift will

propel the Church into greater evangelistic efforts. Revivals, in recent decades, have been reduced to spiritual pep rallies. A return to evangelistic efforts with signs and wonders following will become common again.

The ministry of the apostles and apostolic individuals will help the Church to walk in its former glory and power.

And they went forth, and preached every where, the Lord working with them... (Mark 16:20)

In turn, ministers and believers everywhere will begin to stand up as witnesses of Christ and His resurrection.

Expansion of the Kingdom of God (Baptizing them...)

The apostolic paradigm shift comes to expand the kingdom of God, not to promote apostles and apostolic individuals. Their placement in the Body of Christ is to increase the effectiveness of the Church as it fulfills Christ's commission.

After the Spirit's outpouring, the apostles preached Christ. Moreover, the disciples preached Christ. This resulted in the salvation of many.

Praising God, and having favor with all the people. And the Lord added to the church daily such as should be saved. (Acts 2:47)

The number of converts grew daily. This will be seen today as the apostolic paradigm shift unfolds.

Mature Disciples (Teaching them...)

In Jesus' commission to the disciples, there was a charge to teach men what He commanded. The apostolic company of the apostolic paradigm shift will bring clarity to the mysteries of Christ. Like Paul, they will teach others what Christ has taught them.

> *And they continued steadfastly in the apostles' doctrine and fellowship, and in breaking of bread, and in prayers. (Acts 2:42)*

This results in mature disciples functioning in the Church. The apostolic paradigm shift will produce believers who not only will teach the commands of Christ but walk in those things that are presented.

Greater Faith in the Church (I am with thee always)

To conclude His charge, Jesus gave

the promise of His abiding presence with the disciples. This was to produce faith in them as they went out into a hostile world. In the face of opposition and persecution, they could maintain their resolve to be witnesses of Christ.

> *Behold, I send you forth as sheep in the midst of wolves: be ye therefore wise as serpents, and harmless as doves. (Matthew 10:16)*

Jesus' promise also was to inspire faith in the disciples to expect His supernatural power to accompany them as they ministered in His name. They were to be assured that signs would follow them.

And these signs shall follow them that believe; In my name shall they cast out devils; they shall speak with new tongues; They shall take up serpents; and if they drink any deadly thing, it shall not hurt them; they shall lay hands on the sick, and they shall recover. (Mark 16:20)

The effects of the apostolic paradigm shift will be seen in bold witnessing for Christ. In addition, an increase of the power and demonstration of the Holy Spirit will manifest. It is within the

Great Commission that the apostolic revelation (the Church's revelation and its presentation of Christ) will be fully realized.

Before ending our explanation of the apostolic paradigm shift, we have to address its direct impact on the Body of Christ in particular.

Notes:

THE APOSTOLIC PARRADIGM SHIFT
Examining the Coming Reformation of Apostles and Apostolic Ministry

-Chapter 5-

The Apostolic Reformation

THE APOSTOLIC PARRADIGM SHIFT Examining the Coming Reformation of Apostles and Apostolic Ministry

THE APOSTOLIC PARRADIGM SHIFT
Examining the Coming Reformation of Apostles and Apostolic Ministry

The coming apostolic paradigm shift will affect the Church in various ways. We have established that it will bring hidden apostles and apostolic individuals to the light for Kingdom work. Their work in the Church will set the stage for the end-time outpouring of the Holy Spirit.

This, in turn, will increase the effectiveness of the Church in fulfilling the Great Commission. Yet, there is one final task that the apostolic paradigm shift will perform. It will create an apostolic reformation in the general life of the Church.

The apostolic reformation in the Church will cause the modern-day Church to operate like the early Church. When apostles and apostolic individuals are in place, the authority and anointing of the Church increases.

If we understand the apostolic paradigm shift and embrace the apostolic reformation, we will see the days of Acts repeated presently. The reformation will be seen in three areas:

Reformation of Love

When the apostolic reformation takes place, every believer will operate in love and support of one another. The sign of a true follower of Christ is love. Love, in turn, produces unity.

By this shall all men know that ye are my disciples, if ye have love one to another. (John 13:35)

Since God and Christ are love, the apostolic spirit compels believers to work together in unity. Churches and organizations that are divided over non-essential doctrines will repent and come together.

Reformation of the Miraculous

As the Church embraces the

apostolic reformation, there will be an increase in healing, deliverance, and salvation. The miraculous will be common in the life of the Church.

The least to the greatest among the people will demonstrate the power of God in healing the sick, casting out of devils, and effective evangelism.

> *And these signs shall follow them that believe; In my name shall they cast out devils; they shall speak with new tongues; They shall take up serpents; and if they drink any deadly thing, it shall not hurt them; they*

shall lay hands on the sick, and they shall recover. (Mark 16:17-18)

Reformation of Disciples

The apostolic reformation will cause multiplication in the number of believers and disciples. There is a growing trend of individuals being religious in church without a conversion experience. They are church attendees but not disciples.

The apostolic reformation will cause those in the Church to go beyond religion into discipleship. The Church will grow, not because of religious people, but because souls are added who will be true followers of Christ. In turn, local assemblies will have great impact in their cities, counties, and states because of the apostolic reformation.

And the Lord added to the church daily such as should be saved. (Acts 2:47b)

The apostolic reformation prepares the possessed great power and authority. The apostolic reformation will cause the modern Church to function as they did. If we embrace it, we will see the miraculous of the Books of Acts today. In addition, the Kingdom of God will advance.

THE APOSTOLIC PARRADIGM SHIFT
Examining the Coming Reformation of Apostles and Apostolic Ministry

The apostolic paradigm shift and reformation is upon us. Let us embrace what the Lord is doing in the Church today. In doing so, the Church's authority, anointing, glory, and power will be evident unto all men.

Closing Prayer...

That the God of our Lord Jesus Christ, the Father of glory, may give unto you the spirit of wisdom and revelation in the knowledge of him: The eyes of your understanding being enlightened; that ye may know what is the hope of his calling, and what the riches of the glory of his inheritance in the saints, And what is the exceeding greatness of his power to us-ward who believe, according to the working of his mighty power, Which he wrought in Christ, when he raised him from the dead, and set him at his own right hand in the heavenly places, Far above all principality, and power, and might, and dominion, and every name that is named, not only in this world, but also in that which is to come: And hath put all things under his feet, and gave him to be the head over all things to the church, Which is his body, the fulness of him that filleth all in all. (Ephesians 1:17-23)

THE APOSTOLIC PARRADIGM SHIFT Examining the Coming Reformation of Apostles and Apostolic Ministry

Notes:

THE APOSTOLIC PARRADIGM SHIFT
Examining the Coming Reformation of Apostles and Apostolic Ministry

www.ingramcontent.com/pod-product-compliance
Lightning Source LLC
Chambersburg PA
CBHW050343010526
44119CB00049B/671